Shrubland Birds Survey Fort Necessity National Battlefield: Current Status and Management Recommendations

Technical Report NPS/NER/NRTR—2007/090

Bruce Peterjohn

USGS Patuxent Wildlife Research Center
Laurel, MD 20708

July 2007

U.S. Department of the Interior
National Park Service
Northeast Region
Philadelphia, Pennsylvania

The Northeast Region of the National Park Service (NPS) comprises national parks and related areas in 13 New England and Mid-Atlantic states. The diversity of parks and their resources are reflected in their designations as national parks, seashores, historic sites, recreation areas, military parks, memorials, and rivers and trails. Biological, physical, and social science research results, natural resource inventory and monitoring data, scientific literature reviews, bibliographies, and proceedings of technical workshops and conferences related to these park units are disseminated through the NPS/NER Technical Report (NRTR) and Natural Resources Report (NRR) series. The reports are a continuation of series with previous acronyms of NPS/PHSO, NPS/MAR, NPS/BSO-RNR, and NPS/NERBOST. Individual parks may also disseminate information through their own report series.

Natural Resources Reports are the designated medium for information on technologies and resource management methods; "how to" resource management papers; proceedings of resource management workshops or conferences; and natural resource program descriptions and resource action plans.

Technical Reports are the designated medium for initially disseminating data and results of biological, physical, and social science research that addresses natural resource management issues; natural resource inventories and monitoring activities; scientific literature reviews; bibliographies; and peer-reviewed proceedings of technical workshops, conferences, or symposia.

Mention of trade names or commercial products does not constitute endorsement or recommendation for use by the National Park Service.

This report was accomplished under Interagency Acquisition Agreement F4560040062 with assistance from the NPS. The statements, findings, conclusions, recommendations, and data in this report are solely those of the author(s), and do not necessarily reflect the views of the U.S. Department of the Interior, National Park Service.

Print copies of reports in these series, produced in limited quantity and only available as long as the supply lasts, or preferably, file copies on CD, may be obtained by sending a request to the address on the back cover. Print copies also may be requested from the NPS Technical Information Center (TIC), Denver Service Center, PO Box 25287, Denver, CO 80225-0287. A copy charge may be involved. To order from TIC, refer to document D-070.

This report may also be available as a downloadable portable document format file from the Internet at http://www nps.gov/nero/science/.

Please cite this publication as:

Peterjohn, B. July 2007. Shrubland Birds Survey Fort Necessity National Battlefield: Current Status and Management Recommendations. Technical Report NPS/NER/NRTR—2007/090. National Park Service. Philadelphia, PA.

Table of Contents

Figure

Page

Tables

Summary

Fort Necessity National Battlefield was surveyed for shrubland birds during the 2005 breeding season. While no significant grassland habitats existed in the park, it supported approximately 16.9 ha (41.7 ac) of mixed damp and dry successional habitats in the Great Meadow and 72 ha (177.9 ac) of upland shrubby successional habitats. The natural hydrology of the Great Meadow was altered by drainage and channelization, allowing upland plant communities to invade portions of this former wet meadow. Upland successional habitats were dominated by dense thickets of the invasive Morrow's honeysuckle (*Lonicera morrowii*) and native northern arrow-wood (*Viburnum recognitum*), that apparently inhibit establishment of older successional communities.

These shrublands support breeding bird communities representative of successional habitats within the mountains of southwestern Pennsylvania. The most numerous species include common yellowthroat (*Geothlypis trichas*), eastern towhee (*Pipilo erythrophthalmus*), field sparrow (*Spizella pusilla*), indigo bunting (*Passerina cyanea*), prairie warbler (*Dendroica discolor*), and chestnut-sided warbler (*D. pensylvanica*) in the upland areas. Many of these species, plus yellow warbler (*D. petechia*) and gray catbird (*Dumetella carolinensis*), occur in the Great Meadows. Estimated densities for the most numerous species are comparable to the maximum densities recorded from successional habitats in nearby Maryland. One species of Conservation Concern, the golden-winged warbler (*Vermivora chrysoptera*), was present, although only one territorial male was discovered during the surveys. While existing habitats are suitable to support only a single territory or possibly a small population of golden-winged warblers, management actions that would expand the extent of contiguous shrubland habitats and replace nonnative pine plantations with shrublands dominated by native species could improve the park's habitats for these warblers.

Given the current habitat conditions and management activities, the following recommendations provide the most immediate benefits for breeding shrubland birds in Fort Necessity National Battlefield:

1) Restore natural hydrologic conditions to the Great Meadows, allowing for the reestablishment of wet meadow and shrub-swamp plant communities and the breeding avifauna associated with these communities.

2) Maintain extent and physical structure of shrublands existing in the park. Management activities will be necessary to prevent secondary succession into second-growth woods. Efforts to eliminate invasive shrubs should be combined with intensive management aimed at establishing native shrub communities having similar physical structure.

3) Explore opportunities to expand contiguous shrubland habitats by removing narrow corridors of woods that currently divide upland areas into smaller fragments. The best opportunity is removing wooded habitats separating the Woodcock Field from the Abandoned Orchard/Field, thereby creating a single tract of shrublands >16 ha (40 ac) in extent.

4) Replace nonnative pine plantations with shrubby successional habitats. Wherever nonnative wooded communities are removed, these areas should be allowed to revert to shrubby successional habitats and then maintained at that succesional stage.

Introduction

At the time of European settlement, the status of grassland birds in eastern North America was uncertain. While much of the region was forested, the presence of heath hens (*Tympanuchus cupido cupido*) in a range extending from New England south through the mid-Atlantic states (Forbush 1927) indicates that extensive natural grasslands were present along the Coastal Plain. Grasslands probably existed elsewhere as a result of fire-maintained habitats managed by Native Americans (Askins 2000). These grasslands undoubtedly supported entire communities of grassland birds. As eastern North America was settled by Europeans the original forests were replaced by rural agriculture. and populations of most grassland birds expanded, reaching peak levels during the nineteenth century. Where rural agricultural activities were not economically feasible, however, the farms were replaced by second-growth woodlands. and the first local declines in grassland bird populations occurred (Askins 2000).

During the last decades of the twentieth century grassland birds exhibited the most consistent population declines of any group of North American birds (Peterjohn and Sauer 1999). Anecdotal evidence suggests these declines occurred for nearly a century, prompting considerable concern about the future of these species (Vickery and Herkert 1999; Askins 2000). While the widespread conversion of grasslands into other habitats contributed to these population declines, other factors such as habitat fragmentation and unfavorable mowing regimes were also implicated (Vickery et al. 1999). The plight of grassland birds has heightened awareness of the need for concerted conservation actions to reverse these chronically declining population trends.

While grassland birds have become the focus of increased conservation activities, the status of birds occupying shrubland habitats has received relatively little attention (Hunter et al. 2001). Yet in eastern North America, shrubland birds have also exhibited consistent population declines during the past 40 years (Pardieck and Sauer 2001). These population declines primarily reflect large-scale changes in land use patterns during the previous century. Large areas of marginal farmland were abandoned and underwent secondary succession during the first half of the twentieth century, producing abundant habitats dominated by shrubs and small trees favored by shrubland birds. The maturation of these habitats, combined with fire suppression policies, allowed shrublands to succeed into mature forests, and shrubland bird communities were replaced by woodland birds (Hunter et al. 2001; Lorimer 2001).

The National Park Service (NPS) can potentially contribute to grassland and shrubland bird conservation in the Mid-Atlantic Region. The NPS maintains a number of historic sites and former battlefields managed for their cultural significance with open landscapes, recreating land use patterns existing at the times of the historical events. These open landscapes are frequently managed grasslands that could be maintained to benefit grassland birds, although some parks also support successional habitats that could be managed for shrubland birds.

In 2005, the NPS initiated a project exploring the potential of "cultural parks" to support significant breeding grassland and shrubland bird communities. This project involved parks within three NPS Inventory and Monitoring Program (I&M) networks, Mid-Atlantic, National Capital, and Eastern Rivers and Mountains. Five parks were selected for the focus of this study, all of which maintain open landscapes for interpretation of historic events. Most parks were selected because they represent the most extensive grassland habitats within their networks, although some parks also support significant shrubby successional habitats. The five parks included in this study are: Antietam National Battlefield, Fort Necessity National Battlefield, Gettysburg National Battlefield, Manassas National Battlefield, and Monocacy National Battlefield.

This report summarizes the status of shrubland bird communities on Fort Necessity National Battlefield. The distribution and abundance of breeding shrubland birds were determined from surveys conducted during summer 2005 with the intent of developing parkwide estimates of population sizes. These population estimates are placed within the context of local and regional populations to indicate the relative value of the park for shrubland birds. Results of bird population surveys are combined with the status of current habitat conditions and recent shrubland management strategies to develop recommendations for improving management for shrubland bird populations within the park.

Fort Necessity National Battlefield (FONE) covers approximately 395 ha (976 ac) in three units and is located 17.7 km (11 mi) east of Uniontown in the Alleghany Mountains of Pennsylvania. It is situated in a shallow upland valley between two ridges at elevations of 560-640 m (1,837-2,100 ft) within the Alleghany Plateau physiographic region (Perles et al. 2004). The park is located in a largely rural landscape where residences and small villages are scattered in the valleys while the adjacent ridges are mostly wooded. Shrubland habitats are restricted to one unit (the "Fort Necessity" or main unit) and all bird surveys occurred in there (Figure 1). This unit covers approximately 375 ha (927 ac).

Located within the Youghiogheny River watershed, several small streams traverse the park including Meadow Run that originates just outside the park's boundary and flows through the park's Great Meadow. The Great Meadow was originally an extensive wet meadow meandering through the shallow valley; however, installation of drain tiles and channelization of Meadow Run significantly altered the hydrology of this area and the wet meadow community has been largely replaced by drier upland habitats (Perles et al. 2004). Only 16.9 ha (41.7 ac) of somewhat wet meadow habitat remain.

Perles et al. (2004) documented the plant communities existing within Fort Necessity. The park consists of approximately 280 ha (692 ac) of various woodland communities including Northern Red Oak-Mixed Hardwood Forest, White Oak-Mixed Hardwood Forest, Tulip Poplar Forest, Sugar Maple-Basswood Forest, Modified Successional Forest, and Conifer Plantations. Approximately 72 ha (178 ac) were classified as Successional Old Field communities. These successional habitats include maintained areas around buildings and historic features, and former orchards, pastures, and agricultural fields (Perles et al. 2004).

Vegetative Composition of Shrubby Successional Communities (Perles et al. 2004)

Great Meadow

Wet meadow communities remaining in the Great Meadow consist of dense herbaceous cover approaching 100% of the area with scattered patches of low shrubs covering <30%. The dominant shrubs are meadow-sweet (*Spiraea alba*) and swamp dewberry (*Rubus hispidus*). Dominant herbaceous vegetation include sedges (*Carex* spp., especially *C. stricta*), rough-stemmed goldenrod (*Solidago rugosa*), spike-rushes (*Eleocharis* spp.), rice cutgrass (*Leersia oryzoides*), grass-leaved goldenrod (*Euthamia graminifolia*), soft rush (*Juncus effusus*), and carpet bentgrass (*Agrostis stolonifera*). Herbaceous species associated with upland successional habitats also occur in low abundance.

Upland Successional Habitats

Vegetative composition varies depending upon land use history and the edaphic and moisture characteristics of each site. Trees <20 m (65 ft) in height cover <30% of these habitats. Wild black cherry (*Prunus serotina*), apple (*Malus pumila*), and fanleaf hawthorn (*Crateagus flagellata*) are the most prevalent small trees. A shrub layer 2-6 m (6.5-19.6 ft) tall may cover up

Figure 1. Map of the main unit of Fort Necessity National Battlefield. The Great Meadow survey area is outlined in orange; the Woodcock Field in blue; and the Abandoned Field/Orchard in yellow.

to 80% of these habitats with the dominant species including Morrow's honeysuckle (*Lonicera morrowii*), northern arrow-wood (*Viburnum recognitum*), fanleaf hawthorn, and sweet crabapple (*Malus coronaria*). Shorter shrubs <2 m (6.5 ft) in height generally cover <20% of the area and include Morrow's honeysuckle, northern arrow-wood, dogwoods (*Cornus* spp.), northern dewberry (*Rubus flagellaris*), common blackberry (*R. allegheniensis*), and various young saplings. Vines including poison ivy (*Rhus radicans*) and catbriars (*Smilax* spp.) may cover up to 20% of these habitats. The herbaceous layer tends to be fairly dense and generally covers approximately 85% of the habitats. Grasses dominate this layer during spring and early summer, but goldenrods become prevalent later in the season. The most abundant herbs include rough-stemmed goldenrod, early goldenrod (*Solidago juncea*), grass-leaved goldenrod, carpet bentgrass, sedges, northern oatgrass (*Danthonia compressa*), sweet vernalgrass (*Anthoxanthum odoratum*), deer-tongue grass (*Panicum clandestinum*), velvetgrass (*Holcus lanatus*), and other panic-grasses (*Panicum* spp.).

These habitats are prone to invasion by exotic species. Morrow's honeysuckle is especially prevalent in some areas, while other exotics including multiflora rose (*Rosa multiflora*), Japanese barberry (*Berberis thunbergii*), and crown vetch (*Coronilla varia*) occur in some fields.

Successional habitats tend to be relatively dynamic and vegetative composition changes as one community is replaced by another. No quantitative vegetative surveys were conducted in association with the bird surveys, but qualitative assessment of successional habitat composition indicated few changes to the dominant plant species since the surveys of Perles et al. (2004).

Methods

Yahner et al. (2004) conducted an inventory of Fort Necessity with the goal of identifying 90% of the bird species occurring in the park and determining their breeding status and spatial distributions. Bird inventories consisted of fixed-distance and unlimited-distance point counts, strip transects along habitat edges, vehicular road surveys for diurnal raptors and vultures, and nocturnal surveys for owls. These surveys were conducted throughout the year over a 2-year period. Point count survey sites were randomly selected from a systematic grid system with one point for every 20 ha (49 ac) of acreage. These points were also stratified by major habitat cover type, spatial location (interior vs. edge), and elevation so that the number of points were representative of the habitats within the park. This inventory produced a list of bird species and seasonal measures of relative abundance expressed as mean numbers of birds detected per point (Yahner et al. 2004). These results provide no estimates of total breeding populations for the bird communities occupying shrub-dominated successional habitats.

Shrubland and grassland habitats within Fort Necessity were identified from information provided by the park's resource manager and a visual inspection of the park. Most grasslands were too small (<5 ha [12 ac] in size) to support breeding obligate grassland birds. An area search was conducted on 15 June in the one larger (<10 ha [24 ac]) hayfield, but no obligate grassland birds were noted. Because no grassland birds were present in Fort Necessity during 2005, the bird surveys focused on shrubland habitats. Shrubland bird surveys were conducted during 16 and 27 June 2005. These surveys covered the three largest contiguous tracts of successional habitats in the park: a 6.1 ha (15.1 ac) field managed for American woodcock (*Scolopax minor*) (hereafter, the Woodcock Field), a complex of abandoned fields and orchards totaling 9.8 ha (24.2 ac) (hereafter, the Abandoned Field), and that portion of the Great Meadow not maintained for historic sites and visitor use totaling approximately 6.7 ha (16.6 ac) (hereafter, the Great Meadow) (Figure 1). Edge habitats and narrow shrubby corridors <50 m (164 ft) wide were not surveyed.

These three successional areas were surveyed using the area search methodology of Stewart and Kantrud (1972). The initial survey path was around the perimeter of each field and located 50 m (164 ft) inside and parallel to the field boundary, deviating ±50 m (164 ft) from this path as necessary to adequately survey all habitats and to follow reasonably accessible paths through the dense brushy cover. Smaller fields were surveyed from a single path around the perimeter. In larger fields, additional survey paths were located as necessary inside of the initial path until all habitats were located within 50 m (164 ft) of one survey path. Each area search was conducted until the field was completely surveyed. Survey time generally varied proportionally with field size but was also influenced by field shape and the numbers of birds present. Each field required 1-2 hours to complete the area searches. Walking speeds were normally 2-3 km (1.24-1.86 mi) per hour but could vary depending on the number of birds present in a field.

Surveys were focused on birds occupying these shrubby successional habitats. Birds associated with wooded edges or other non-shrubland habitats, habitat generalists such as crows (*Corvus* spp.), and aerial insectivores were not included in the surveys. When encountered during area searches, each shrubland bird was identified to species and gender whenever possible based on plumage and/or behavioral traits. When gender could not be positively assigned in the field, individuals were classified as unknown. Each time an individual bird was detected it was also recorded, up to a maximum of five detections. One "detection" was defined as a distinct vocal cue such as a song or call note, or visual cues such as a bird observed on a perch or in flight.

The area search methodology was intended to survey shrublands as thoroughly as possible, but some shrubland birds were undoubtedly missed during these surveys. The Chao 1 (bias corrected) estimator (Chao 1984) was used to develop population estimates that incorporated estimates of birds present but not detected during the surveys. Numbers of individuals noted by one detection and two detections were input into the Chao 1 formulas to develop estimates of total population size, variance, and 95% confidence intervals for the more numerous species. Species represented by small numbers lacked sufficient sample sizes to use the Chao 1 estimator; for these species the observed totals are presented without correction for detectability.

Results

Survey results from the three shrubby successional fields are provided in Table 1. Breeding birds are fairly numerous in each field; however, the composition and relative abundance of species varies in response to shrub height, shrub density, hydrologic conditions, and other factors. These bird communities are briefly described below:

Great Meadow

Twelve species of breeding birds were recorded in this area, a community composed of species that occupy dry upland and more mesic habitats. The most numerous species were gray catbird (*Dumetella carolinensis*), yellow warbler (*Dendroica petechia*), common yellowthroat (*Geothlypis trichas*), song sparrow (*Melospiza melodia*), and indigo bunting (*Passerina cyanea*). A few birds prefer the more poorly drained portions of the Great Meadow, the only location for willow flycatcher (*Empidonax traillii*) and swamp sparrow (*Melospiza georgiana*) in the park; while gray catbirds and yellow warblers are decidedly more numerous in these mesic habitats than in the drier uplands. The upland species were generally more numerous in other habitats within the park.

Table 1. Total numbers of breeding shrubland birds recorded during area search surveys of Fort Necessity National Battlefield during 16 and 27 June 2005.

Species Common Name (*Scientific Name*)	Abandoned Field	Woodcock Field	Great Meadows
ring-necked pheasant (*Phasianus colchicus*)	1 M		
yellow-billed cuckoo (*Coccyzus americanus*)	1 U		
ruby-throated hummingbird (*Archilochus colubris*)	1 U	1 M	
willow flycatcher (*Empidonax traillii*)			1 U
white-eyed vireo (*Vireo griseus*)	1 M	3 M	
gray catbird (*Dumetella carolinensis*)		1 M	6 M; 2 U
brown thrasher (*Toxostoma rufum*)	1 U	2 M; 2 U	1 M
golden-winged warbler (*Vermivora chrysoptera*)	1 M		
yellow warbler (*Dendroica petechia*)	1 M		6 M
chestnut-sided warbler (*Dendroica pensylvanica*)	8 M; 1 F	7 M	
prairie warbler (*Dendroica discolor*)	5 M	9 M; 2 F	
black-and-white warbler (*Mniotilta varia*)		1 F	
common yellowthroat (*Geothlypis trichas*)	18 M	10 M	6 M
yellow-breasted chat (*Icteria virens*)	3 M; 2 U	2 M; 1 U	
eastern towhee (*Pipilo erythrophthalmus*)	12 M; 3 F	12 M; 2 F	5 M
chipping sparrow (*Spizella passerina*)		1 U	
field sparrow (*Spizella pusilla*)	7 M; 2 U	3 M; 6 U	2 M
song sparrow (*Melospiza melodia*)	5 M	3 M	6 M; 4 F
swamp sparrow (*Melospiza georgiana*)			1 M; 3 U
northern cardinal (*Cardinalis cardinalis*)	2 M; 1 U	1 M	1 M
indigo bunting (*Passerina cyanea*)	11 M; 1 F	8 M	8 M
red-winged blackbird (*Agelaius phoeniceus*)			2 M; 1 F

M = males
F = females
U = unknown gender

Woodcock Field

A total of 15 species of breeding birds occupied the dense shrubby habitats along this fairly dry hillside. Eastern towhee (*Pipilo erythrophthalmus*), common yellowthroat, prairie warbler (*Dendroica discolor*), indigo bunting, field sparrow (*Spizella pusilla*), and chestnut-sided warbler (*Dendroica pensylvanica*) dominated the breeding avifauna in this area.

Abandoned Field/Orchard

Despite a greater prevalence of small trees, this area supported a similar breeding avifauna as the Woodcock Field. This community totaled 16 species. While common yellowthroats were most numerous, the other dominant birds included those noted in the Woodcock Field, except for smaller numbers of prairie warblers.

Composition of these shrubland bird communities is similar to those found along the Allegheny Mountains in southwestern Pennsylvania (Brauning 1992). No species were unexpectedly absent, while one species of Conservation Concern was detected during these surveys.

Golden-winged Warbler (*Vermivora chrysoptera*)

A singing male golden-winged warbler was discovered in the Abandoned Field/Orchard during the 16 June survey. This male sang repeatedly from multiple perches within the lower portion of the field, indicating that the bird was probably on territory. No mate was discovered, but silent females are difficult to detect in dense shrubby cover. This bird could not be located during 27 June, but if this male were not singing, then it would be very difficult to locate within the dense cover.

Breeding golden-winged warblers occupy dense shrubby habitats with scattered young saplings but disappear when a closed canopy develops. They prefer mesic habitats but also occur in somewhat drier upland areas (Confer 1992). In Pennsylvania, these warblers most frequently occur at elevations above 304 m (1,000 ft). They are most numerous in the central Appalachian Mountain portion of the Ridge and Valley physiographic region and in the Pocono Mountains. These warblers were widely distributed across southwestern Pennsylvania during the 1980s (Brauning 1992). Whether this status has changed during recent years is uncertain.

Golden-winged warbler is a species of Conservation Concern—reflecting its relatively small population size, limited breeding distribution, and significantly declining population trends during the past 50 years (Confer 1992). Habitat loss has contributed to golden-winged warbler population declines, especially in areas where successional habitats have been largely replaced by second-growth woods. Other factors, however, are also likely involved. Whenever blue-winged warblers (*Dendroica pinus*) move into an area occupied by golden-winged warblers, the latter species invariably disappears (Gill 1980). Whether the disappearance of golden-winged warblers results from hybridization, is due to competition, or some combination of these and other factors is uncertain (Confer and Knapp 1981). But as the breeding range of blue-winged warblers expands, the range of golden-winged warblers has retreated northward and into higher elevations where blue-winged warblers are absent.

Population estimates for shrubland birds in Fort Necessity are provided in Table 2. The breeding avifauna was relatively dense in most shrubland habitats with density estimates exceeding one male per hectare for common yellowthroat, eastern towhee, and indigo bunting and approached one male per hectare for chestnut-sided and prairie warblers. Breeding birds were more numerous in upland habitats than in the mesic shrublands of the Great Meadow.

Table 2. Population estimates, expressed in numbers of territorial males, for shrubland birds on Fort Necessity National Battlefield during June 2005. Ninety-five percent confidence intervals for population estimates are provided when sufficient sample sizes allow (see Methods for details).

Species	Population Estimate	Density (males/ha)
ring-necked pheasant	1	0.10
yellow-billed cuckoo	1	0.10
ruby-throated hummingbird	2	0.13
willow flycatcher	1	0.15
white-eyed vireo	4	0.25
gray catbird	7	0.55
brown thrasher	4	0.18
golden-winged warbler	1	0.10
yellow warbler	7	0.42
chestnut-sided warbler	15.3 ± 0.9	0.96
prairie warbler	15.5 ± 6.7	0.97
black-and-white warbler	1	0.10
common yellowthroat	34.3 ± 0.4	1.52
yellow-breasted chat	5	0.31
eastern towhee	29.7 ± 1.3	1.31
chipping sparrow	1	0.16
field sparrow	12.8 ± 2.0[1]	0.57
song sparrow	14.2 ± 0.4[1]	0.63
swamp sparrow	2	0.30
northern cardinal	4	0.18
indigo bunting	28.7 ± 4.9	1.27
red-winged blackbird	2	0.30

[1]Detections of these species included a number of individuals that could not be assigned to gender. These estimates are probably low compared to other species where all males could be readily identified.

Discussion

Fort Necessity supports an abundant and reasonably diverse shrubland bird community representative of the Allegheny Plateau region of southwestern Pennsylvania (Brauning 1992). Most species are widely distributed across the region; hence, numbers of breeding pairs present in Fort Necessity represent only a tiny percentage of county or regional populations. The park currently provides habitat for one species of Conservation Concern, the golden-winged warbler. Only one territorial male was noted during 2005. Additional surveys should be considered in the future to determine if the observation of this single male was a chance event or if a small population may still persist in the park. Because this species avoids successional areas (<2 ha [5 ac]) and prefers patches >12 ha (30 ac) in extent (Hunter et al. 2001), the shrubby successional habitats currently available in Fort Necessity are not likely to support a sizable breeding population. Maintaining existing successional habitats, combined with habitat enhancements, however, may allow the park to support larger numbers of breeding golden-winged warblers.

Shrubland bird densities within Fort Necessity are comparable to those reported from other shrubby successional habitats in the region. The most numerous species exhibited densities of approximately 1-1.5 territorial males per ha that approach the maximum densities reported for chestnut-sided warbler, prairie warbler, common yellowthroat, eastern towhee, and indigo bunting in Maryland (Robbins and Blom 1996).

Breeding behavior was widely noted during the June surveys. Observations of adults' behavior suggested that many pairs were feeding young in the nest during 16 June, although relatively few young had fledged by that date. Many young-of-the-year were evident on 27 June. While detailed studies of reproductive success were not conducted, the numbers of young birds observed in these habitats suggests these habitats may be sources and not necessarily population sinks within the source-sink population dynamics described by Pulliam (1988).

Historic alterations to the hydrology of the Great Meadow have influenced the composition of its breeding avifauna. While some species characteristic of shrub-swamp wetlands occur there, the bird community is dominated by species preferring mesic or upland habitats. If the original natural conditions were restored, changes would be evident in the breeding avifauna. Upland birds, such as indigo buntings and song sparrows, would decline in abundance, while species preferring wetter areas, such as willow flycatchers, yellow warblers, and swamp sparrows, would probably become more numerous. An extensive wet meadow/shrub swamp could attract additional species that do not currently occur in Fort Necessity, such as alder flycatchers (*Empidonax alnorum*), and possibly some marsh birds, including rails and bitterns. Damp shrubby areas along the margins could provide more extensive breeding habitats for golden-winged warblers and could contribute to a larger breeding population within the park.

Upland successional habitats support a relatively diverse breeding avifauna despite their domination by Morrow's honeysuckle and other invasive shrubs. The shrubby cover tends to be very dense, especially in the Woodcock Field, which may inhibit establishment of native saplings and retard secondary succession into second-growth woods. Hence, these communities dominated by invasives may be more resilient to successional changes than upland shrublands dominated by native species. Additionally, the honeysuckle, northern arrow-wood, crabapples, dogwoods, blackberries, and other species produce abundant fruit crops that are used heavily by birds during the breeding season and other times of the year. These shrubby successional habitats may also provide important post-breeding foraging and molting locations for woodland birds (Vega Rivera et al. 1999; Pagen et al. 2000).

Recommendations

The following recommendations are intended to improve the management of Fort Necessity for breeding shrubland birds. These recommendations represent the opinions of the author as supported by the cited literature. The conceptual model for managing shrubland birds in cultural parks (Peterjohn 2006) should be consulted for additional information on management activities related to the following recommendations.

Restore Natural Hydrologic Conditions to the Great Meadow

Restoring natural hydrology to the Great Meadow would expand the extent of wetlands in the park and increase overall habitat diversity. These actions would also restore habitats closer to the conditions existing at the time of the battle. Upland successional communities existing in the Great Meadow would most likely disappear and be replaced initially by wet grasslands and eventually by a shrub swamp community. Birds associated with upland habitats would disappear or be forced to the margins of the wetlands, while birds preferring wetland habitats should become prevalent.

These activities could also benefit golden-winged warblers breeding in the park. This species prefers mesic shrubby habitats that will eventually become established in most of the area (Confer 1992); although, the species may be absent during the initial years when these habitats are dominated by herbaceous vegetation. While the result would likely be an increase in the numbers of golden-winged warblers breeding in Fort Necessity, the restored Great Meadow would still be too small to support a sizable population.

Where second-growth woods have encroached on the Great Meadow, these woodlands could be removed to restore the area to its original extent. These activities would increase the extent of successional habitats available within the park while a larger Great Meadow area would attract a larger number and variety of breeding birds.

Maintain Extent and Physical Structure of Shrublands Existing in the Park

Successional habitats are normally ephemeral with each community creating conditions under which the next successional stage can develop. Given the dynamic nature of succession, maintaining shrubland communities for prolonged periods of time is very difficult to achieve. For areas that currently support shrubby successional communities, the park should prevent these areas from advancing into second-growth woods. In order to maintain the shrubby character of these habitats as much as possible, these management activities should involve the periodic selective removal of emergent saplings and other taller woody vegetation. Although labor intensive, hand removal of saplings combined with the chemical treatment of stumps to prevent re-sprouting is the most effective approach to maintain shrub-dominated communities (Askins 2001; Thompson and DeGraaf 2001).

From the perspective of shrubland birds, the existing habitats provide abundant food and dense cover. While birds are numerous in these habitats dominated by invasive shrubs, the NPS normally eliminates invasive species from its parks whenever possible.

Given their prevalence in these habitats, eliminating invasive species will cause major changes to these shrubland communities. After the dominant invasives have been eliminated keeping other invasive plants from becoming established will require considerable effort and resources. Because the dominant invasive species may be preventing the widespread establishment of saplings, eliminating the invasives may allow saplings to become established and promote succession into second-growth woods. Hence, any attempt at the widespread elimination of invasive shrubs will likely result in major changes to these shrubland communities and to the birds that currently occupy these habitats. Additionally, the fruits of many invasive shrubs are dispersed by birds, and preventing these invasives from becoming re-established will likely require considerable effort.

An alternative approach to eliminating all invasive shrubs at once is removing invasives from relatively small areas (<0.5 ha [1.2 ac]) followed by the immediate planting of native species such as northern arrow-wood, dogwoods, northern dewberry, and other species that can establish dense shrubby cover similar to the existing habitats. Intensive management will likely be necessary to prevent reestablishment of invasives—activities that will likely be required for several years. Once the native community is fairly well established and less management is necessary, then another area can undergo similar treatment and re-planting. This approach would maintain the dense vegetative structure characteristic of existing habitats and retain most birds that currently use these habitats, yet result in the eventual elimination of invasive species. These native shrubs also produce an abundant berry crop during most years that would be attractive for a variety of shrubland and woodland birds following the breeding season.

Explore Opportunities to Expand Contiguous Shrubland Habitats

The selective removal of second-growth, wooded habitats could expand the extent of contiguous shrubland habitats in the park. For example, a fairly narrow wooded area currently separates the Woodcock Field from the Abandoned Field/Orchard. Removing these wooded habitats would create a single tract of successional habitats 16 ha (>40 ac) in extent. Shrubby successional habitats of this size are more favorable for establishing populations of golden-winged warblers and other shrubland birds that prefer large contiguous tracts of successional habitats (Hunter et al. 2001). Other shrubland birds may prefer these larger tracts of successional habitats (Annand and Thompson 1997), but area sensitivity is not as well established for shrubland birds as for grassland species (Krementz and Christie 2000).

Removing additional narrow, wooded corridors could allow these upland successional areas to become contiguous with the Great Meadow, greatly expanding the extent of contiguous shrublands within the park. However, these management activities may conflict with the goal of maintaining habitats as they existed at the time of the historical event, because the Great Meadow would have been bordered by woodlands and not by successional habitats during the eighteenth century.

Replace Nonnative Pine Plantations with Shrubby Successional Habitats

Several small plantations of nonnative pines (*Pinus* spp.) exist within the park. If these habitats are removed in an attempt to restore native plant communities within Fort Necessity, allowing these areas to revert to shrubby successional habitats would increase the extent of these habitats.

16

Even if these sites are relatively small (<3 ha [7.4 ac]), they would still be occupied by most breeding birds observed in shrubby successional habitats elsewhere in Fort Necessity.

Literature Cited

Annand, M. E., and F. R. Thompson, III. 1997. Forest bird response to regeneration practices in central hardwood forests. Journal of Wildlife Management 61:159-171.

Askins, R. A. 2000. Restoring North American's birds, lessons from landscape ecology. Yale University Press. New Haven, CT.

Askins, R. A. 2001. Sustaining biological diversity in early successional communities: the challenge of managing unpopular habitats. Wildlife Society Bulletin 29:407-412.

Brauning, D. W., ed. 1992. Atlas of breeding birds in Pennsylvania. University of Pittsburgh Press. Pittsburgh, PA.

Chao, A. 1984. Non-parametric estimation of the number of classes in a population. Scandinavian Journal of Statistics 11:265-270.

Confer, J. L. 1992. Golden-winged Warbler (*Vermivora chrysoptera*). *In* The Birds of North America, No. 20. A. Poole, P. Stettenheim, and F. Gill, eds. The Birds of North America Inc. Philadelphia, PA.

Confer, J. L., and K. Knapp. 1981. Golden-winged and Blue-winged Warblers: the relative success of a habitat specialist and a generalist. Auk 98:108-114.

Forbush, E. H. 1927. Birds of Massachusetts and other New England states. Norwood Press. Norwood, MA.

Gill, F. B. 1980. Historical aspects of hybridization between Blue-winged and Golden-winged Warblers. Auk 97:1-18.

Hunter, W. C., D. A. Buehler, R. A. Canterbury, J. L. Confer, and P. B. Hamel. 2001. Conservation of disturbance-dependent birds in eastern North America. Wildlife Society Bulletin 29:440-455.

Krementz, D. G., and J. S. Christie. 2000. Clearcut stand size and scrub-successional bird assemblages. Auk 117:913-924.

Lorimer, C. G. 2001. Historical and ecological roles of disturbance in eastern North American forests: 9,000 years of change. Wildlife Society Bulletin 29:425-439.

Pagen, R. W., F. R. Thompson, III., and D. E. Burhans. 2000. Breeding and post-breeding habitat use by forest migrant songbirds in the Missouri Ozarks. Condor 102:738-747.

Pardieck, K. L., and J. R. Sauer. 2001. The 1995-99 summary of the North American Breeding Bird Survey. Bird Populations 5:30-48.

Perles, S. J., G. S. Podniesinksi, and E. A. Zimmerman. 2004. Vegetation community classification and mapping at Fort Necessity National Battlefield. Report prepared for the National Park Service,. Northeast Region. Philadelphia, PA.

Peterjohn, B. G. 2006. Conceptual ecological model for management of breeding shrubland birds in the mid-Atlantic region. Technical Report NPS/NER/NRTR 2006/043. National Park Service. Philadelphia, PA.

Peterjohn, B. G., and J. R. Sauer. 1999. Population status of North American grassland birds from the North American Breeding Bird Survey, 1966-1996. Studies in Avian Biology 19:27-44.

Pulliam, H. R. 1988. Sources, sinks, and population regulation. American Naturalist 132:652-661.

Robbins, C. S., and E. A. T. Blom. 1996. Atlas of the Breeding Birds of Maryland and the District of Columbia. University of Pittsburgh Press. Pittsburgh, PA.

Stewart, R. E., and H. A. Kantrud. 1972. Population estimates of breeding birds in North Dakota. The Auk 89:766-788.

Thompson, III., F. R., and R. M. DeGraaf. 2001. Conservation approaches for woody, early successional communities in the southeastern United States. Wildlife Society Bulletin 29:483-494.

Vega Rivera, J. H., W. J. McShea, J. H. Rappole, and C. A. Haas. 1999. Postbreeding movements and habitat use of adult Wood Thrushes in northern Virginia. Auk 116:450-466.

Vickery, P. D., and J. R. Herkert, eds. 1999. Ecology and conservation of grassland birds of the western hemisphere. Studies in Avian Biology No. 19.

Vickery, P. D., P. L. Tubaro, J. M. Cardosa da Silva, B. G. Peterjohn, J. R. Herkert, and R. B. Cavalcanti. 1999. Conservation of grassland birds in the Western Hemisphere. Studies in Avian Biology 19:2-26.

Yahner, R. H., B. D. Ross, and J. E. Kubel. 2004. Comprehensive inventory of birds and mammals at Fort Necessity National Battlefield and Friendship Hill National Historic Site. Technical Report NPS/NERCHAL/NRTR-04/093. National Park Service. Philadelphia, PA.

As the nation's primary conservation agency, the Department of the Interior has responsibility for most of our nationally owned public land and natural resources. This includes fostering sound use of our land and water resources; protecting our fish, wildlife, and biological diversity; preserving the environmental and cultural values of our national parks and historical places; and providing for the enjoyment of life through outdoor recreation. The department assesses our energy and mineral resources and works to ensure that their development is in the best interests of all our people by encouraging stewardship and citizen participation in their care. The department also has a major responsibility for American Indian reservation communities and for people who live in island territories under U.S. administration.

NPS D-70 July 2007

National Park Service
U.S. Department of the Interior

Northeast Region
Natural Resource Stewardship and Science
200 Chestnut Street
Philadelphia, Pennsylvania 19106-2878

http://www.nps.gov/nero/science/

www.ingramcontent.com/pod-product-compliance
Lightning Source LLC
Chambersburg PA
CBHW080937290526
45795CB00007BA/2795